Rosa Parks
and her Protest for
Civil Rights
1 December 1955

Rosa Parks
and her Protest for
Civil Rights
1 December 1955

CHERRYTREE BOOKS

A Cherrytree Book

This edition published in 2007
by Cherrytree Books, part of
The Evans Publishing Group
2A Portman Mansions
Chiltern Street
London W1U 6NR

Reprinted 2009

VISIT OUR WEBSITE
www.evansbooks.co.uk
Evans

British Library Cataloguing in Publication Data

Philip, Steele, 1948 -
  Rosa Parks and her protest for civil rights. - (Dates with
  history)
  1.Parks, Rosa, 1913- 2.African American civil rights
  workers - Alabama - Montgomery - Biography - Juvenile
  literature 3.Civil rights movements - United States -
  Juvenile literature
  I.Title
  323'.092

ISBN 9781842344064

Printed in China by WKT Co.Ltd.

Picture credits:
AFP: 26
Corbis: Front cover, 6, 9, 11, 16, 17, 20, 21, 24, 25, 27
Hulton Getty: 8, 10, 13, 14, 15, 22, 2
Topham Picturepoint: 12, 18, 19

Contents

Dreaming of a fairer world

Decembwer 1955: Christmas is coming, the season of goodwill. Shops are beginning to put up coloured lights and sparkling trees. This is Montgomery, state capital of Alabama, in the heart of the American South. The city made its name as a market for cotton, timber and cattle, but it has grown in recent years.

Montgomery's pavements are busy this evening with workers returning home. Many of them are **African Americans**. Although they make up over a third of the city's population of 130,000, they are treated as second-class citizens by most of the whites who live there. Among the blacks is Rosa Parks, tired after a hard day's work at her sewing machine. She is a quiet middle-aged woman, who hasn't stood out in the crowd, until now.

Rosa was born Rosa Louise McCauley in Tuskegee, Alabama on 4 February 1913. She knew poverty and hard times at an early

Rosa Parks in the 1950s.

age. Her father was James McCauley, a carpenter and stonemason. Her mother was a teacher called Leona Edwards. Both were African Americans. Rosa was given a strict Christian upbringing in the African Methodist Episcopal Church.

At the Montgomery Industrial School for Girls, aged 11, Rosa was no rebel. She was serious, quietly spoken and did as she was told. However her parents did tell her about African American history and of their dreams for a fairer world.

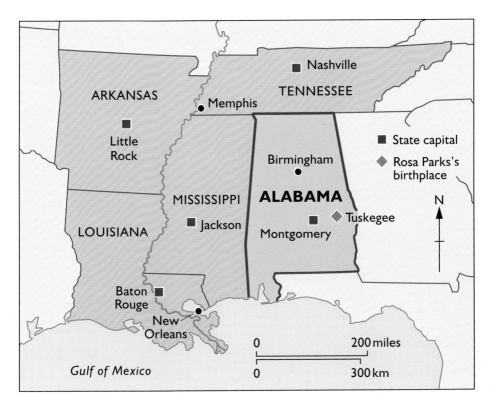

A map showing Alabama and neighbouring southern states of the USA.

Rosa's refusal

In 1932 Rosa married a barber called Raymond Parks. Raymond and Rosa shared a passion for social justice and during this time both campaigned for the National Association for the Advancement of Colored People (NAACP). Through this organisation, Rosa met both blacks and whites who were determined to bring about a fairer society.

A woman recruits new members for the NAACP in the 1950s.

After finishing work on 1 December 1955, Rosa boards the bus and buys a ticket. The front of the bus is reserved for whites. Blacks must sit at the back. Blacks are allowed to sit in the middle, but only if no whites are left standing. Rosa sits in the middle.

Rosa hates this **discrimination** against her people. Back in 1943 she had an argument with a racist bus driver over this. She now realises that this same man, James F Blake, is driving the bus this evening. At the third stop a white man climbs aboard and demands a seat in the middle section. Driver Blake orders all the blacks in Rosa's row to stand. The others begin to obey – but Rosa refuses to move. Blake calls the police. When they arrive, they arrest Rosa. The prisoner goes peacefully, is taken to the police station and fingerprinted. Some days later, she is fined $10.

The NAACP is angry that Rosa has been humiliated in this way and decides to **boycott** the public transport system. Seventy-five per cent of the city's bus passengers are black. Let the bus company see how they survive without these fares. The word spreads like wildfire among African Americans. Walk, organise lifts, ride bicycles – but don't travel by bus!

Rosa Parks photographed sitting at the front of a bus after her protest in 1955.

A change in the law

Activists set up the Montgomery Improvement Association (MIA) to organise the protest. Its elected leader is the **pastor** of the Baptist church on Dexter Avenue, Dr Martin Luther King Junior. He is a captivating speaker, whom Rosa has already met. The MIA's demands are modest: that courtesy is shown to black passengers, that blacks no longer have to give up their seats, that the bus company hires black drivers.

Martin Luther King standing outside his church when he was pastor.

Martin Luther King and Glenn Smiley sit next to each other on a bus in 1956.

Rosa campaigns tirelessly and loses her job because of her efforts. Many African Americans are beaten up and arrested. King's home is bombed. But the boycott holds out until 13 November 1956, when the US Supreme Court finally rules that Alabama's transport laws are illegal. On 21 December 1956 Martin Luther King and a white minister named Glenn Smiley sit side-by-side on a bus. Rosa has won her battle.

Rosa Parks had started a new chapter in the story of African Americans and their campaign for civil rights. What lay behind her brave protest? What was the history of African Americans and why were they treated so unfairly?

Out of slavery

Slavery has been common throughout history. Slaves are people who are bought and sold like property and forced to work for no wages. Europeans took part in the West African slave trade from the 1500s, shipping slaves to the new lands of the Americas. The slaves were kept in chains, and thrown overboard if they became sick.

A rich landowner buying black slaves.

The slaves who survived the Atlantic crossing were landed on the Caribbean islands or on the North American mainland. Individuals were sold and branded like cattle and forced to work on large farming estates, called **plantations**. They toiled in the hot sun, hoeing or harvesting cotton.

Punishments were harsh, with slaves being whipped, hanged and even burnt alive. Most white people at that time believed that whites were superior to blacks. However, some whites did recognise that these beliefs were **immoral**. After the USA became independent from Britain (1775-1783) the northern states abandoned the use of slave labour, but this did not happen in the South.

Black slaves picking cotton in the fields of Texas.

Britain halted the Atlantic slave trade in 1807 and abolished slavery throughout its huge empire, including the Caribbean region, in 1833. In the same year, the American Anti-Slavery Society called for the **abolition** of slavery throughout the USA.

In 1861 the northern and southern states engaged in a terrible **Civil War**. The Union (northern) side supported the end of slavery. The southern Confederacy – first set up in Montgomery, Alabama – supported slavery. About 179,000 African American troops fought for the Union, which finally won in 1865, and slavery was abolished.

Segregation and terror

After the Civil War, freed slaves looked forward to a bright future, but once the northern troops had withdrawn from the South, old injustices were recreated.

In 1888 the first segregation laws were passed in Mississippi and blacks were no longer able to mix with whites. Other laws made it impossible for most blacks to qualify to vote in elections. These became known as 'Jim Crow' laws, after a mocking dance called 'Jump, Jim Crow', performed by 'blacked-up' white entertainers.

The Rex Theatre in Mississippi, which was segregated under the 'Jim Crow' laws.

In 1866 a white racist terror group was founded, called the Ku Klux Klan. Its members murdered and tortured thousands of blacks. In 1915 the Klan was revived, attracting new members across the USA. Rosa Parks's childhood was haunted by terrifying 'Klansmen' marching up and down her street, threatening black families.

Blacks in the South were little better off than in the days of slavery. Many lived in poor, country shacks with few possessions. The cotton fields offered tough, blistering, poorly paid work. Rosa picked cotton as a child, for 50 cents a day. Many poor whites were little better off than the blacks. During the 1930s, both peoples suffered greatly during a period of severe unemployment, known as the Great Depression.

Cloaked and hooded members of the Ku Klux Klan group standing in front of a fiery cross – one of their symbols.

This ended with the Second World War (1939-45). Although the war was being fought against German racists, black troops still suffered from discrimination in the US armed forces.

The struggle for black rights

African American campaigns for civil rights had already been going on for 50 years or more, when Rosa Parks made her protest in 1955. The NAACP had been founded as early as 1909. In 1934 an African American Moslem called Elijah Muhammad had set up a black separatist movement known as the Nation of Islam.

Paul Robeson was a football star, a lawyer, a world-famous singer, an actor and a film star.

After the Second World War, black rights were championed by a remarkable African American called Paul Robeson. In the 1950s, Robeson lost work as the US government accused him of being a **communist** trouble-maker. The same accusation would soon be levelled against Rosa Parks during the bus boycott.

In August 1955, Rosa Parks was shocked and saddened by the murder of a black teenager called Emmett Till. Emmett had come down from Chicago to visit relatives in Money, Mississippi. He boasted to friends that he had dated a white girl back home. They dared him to chat to the white woman who ran the local store, Carolyn Bryant. When he called her 'baby', she complained to her husband that Emmett had spoken without due respect.

Emmett was seized by Carolyn's husband and brother, tortured, shot and thrown into the Tallahatchie River. When the case came to trial, the Ku Klux Klan **intimidated** witnesses. An all-white **jury** found the murderers 'not guilty'.

Black teenager Emmett Till in 1955.

Death threats and protests

The civil rights movement was growing across the USA, with the support of young blacks and whites. Blacks were encouraged to register to vote. A growing threat came from racist White Citizens' Councils. These were made up of 'respectable' citizens, but they did everything they could to oppose justice for blacks. In 1957 Rosa Parks received one death threat too many. She and Raymond moved north to Detroit, Michigan.

Members of the sheriff's mounted posse patrol the front of the bus station in Montgomery, Alabama, following the arrival of a group of 'Freedom Riders'.

In 1960 black students in Nashville, Tennessee, sat down at a lunch counter in a department store, which was reserved for whites. They refused to move. This was just the first of many 'sit-in protests'. In 1961 two buses of blacks and whites set out from Washington, DC, for New Orleans. They wished to challenge segregation on inter-state buses. In Alabama these 'Freedom Riders' were fire-bombed and beaten up. The state governor took no action. Eventually the US Attorney-General Robert Kennedy stepped in, to enforce inter-state bus **integration**.

A black student is protected by a US marshal as she walks to college.

Another civil rights battlefield was education. Segregation in schools had been banned in 1954, but this law was ignored in the South.

In 1957 black pupils admitted to the all-white high school in Little Rock, Arkansas, were met by an angry white mob and paratroops had to be called in to protect them.

19

'I have a dream. . .'

The year 1963 saw the civil rights movement at its height, but it was a year of tragedy. On 12 June Medgar Evers, NAACP secretary in Mississippi, was gunned down in front of his home. He had campaigned for voter registration and for the boycott of whites-only stores. It was he who had helped organise witnesses in the Emmett Till murder trial.

During the 1963 Freedom March, King spoke about discrimination in both northern and southern states.

Evers's murder led to a meeting between civil rights workers and US President John F Kennedy, who now called for new laws. On 22 November 'JFK', who was idolised by many progressive young Americans, was assassinated in Dallas, Texas. To this day, nobody is sure why.

On 23 June 1963 Rosa Parks who, by now, was a prominent figure among civil rights activists, and Martin Luther King led a Great March to Freedom through the streets of Detroit. Two months later Rosa Parks joined the vast stream of people marching on Washington, DC.

Some 300,000 people gathered at the centre of the capital. Rosa was angry that no women were asked to address the crowd, but Martin Luther King made a very moving speech which went down in history. He began with the words 'I have a dream...'

In 1965 Rosa Parks gave up her sewing job and started to work for John Conyers, an African American who had been elected as Congressman.

In March of that year another march started out in Alabama, from Selma to Montgomery. The marchers were calling for black voting rights to be protected. But the peaceful marchers were brutally attacked by police and state troopers. Rosa was anguished. She flew to Montgomery where, with Martin Luther King, she addressed 25,000 protestors.

In his famous 'I have a dream' speech, Martin Luther King described his vision of an America free from racial injustice.

Black Power

Dr Martin Luther King was by now known and respected around the world. In 1964 he was awarded the **Nobel Peace Prize**. Despite all the violence directed at him, King never returned the hatred and campaigned using only non-violent methods. On 4 April 1968 King was assassinated. He was killed by a white racist called James Earl Ray, in Tennessee.

On 5 June another assassination shocked the USA. The victim was Robert Kennedy, brother of JFK and supporter of the civil rights campaign. Rosa Parks was shattered by the loss of two men whom she had so admired.

National guardsmen patrol the streets after the Detroit riots in 1967 (see page 23).

Over time the non-violent methods preached by Martin Luther King achieved some success. Major political reforms were brought in during the 1960s. However young blacks were growing restless. Political change had brought no **economic** benefits. Blacks still lived in poor housing. They still could not get decent jobs. They were expected to fight for their country in the Vietnam War, but at home they were still **harassed** by the police.

Between 1964 and 1967 there were riots in cities across the USA. Many people died, hundreds were injured, thousands were left homeless. Rosa Parks sharply condemned the rioting, even if she understood its causes. However, many young blacks declared that violence had to be met with violence. Many called for revolution and **Black Power**. An armed revolutionary organisation called the Black Panthers was founded and there was even a Black Power protest at the 1968 Olympic Games, in Mexico.

Malcolm X was murdered by former comrades in 1965.

Rosa Parks, the gentle Christian activist, belonged to a different generation. But even she respected one of the new leaders, Malcolm 'X', when she met him. He founded a new Organisation for Afro-American Unity, calling for peace.

Change for the better. . . and worse

Many of the older civil rights activists were bitterly disappointed by the violent mood of the late 1960s and 70s, but they understood how young African Americans felt angry and frustrated.

Black athlete Carl Lewis gained the respect of the nation when he won four gold medals in the 1984 Olympic Games.

The 1980s and 90s did see a great change in public attitudes in the USA. Black stars were now to be seen on films and television. Black musicians, athletes, poets and writers were respected by both blacks and whites. African Americans entered politics and business. By 1989 there was even a black state governor in Mississippi. A national holiday in January was declared to honour Martin Luther King.

For all these gains, there were worrying signs that the goals of Rosa Parks and other civil rights campaigners had still not been met.

Police officer Powell (right) with his family during his trial for assaulting Rodney King.

In 1991 a video recording showed two police officers kicking and beating up a black motorist, Rodney King, in Los Angeles. The policemen were acquitted, although a re-trial found both of them guilty. In 1998 a disabled black man from the South, James Byrd, was chained to back of a truck and dragged along the road until he died.

The Ku Klax Klan still existed, only its members now wore smart suits and talked politely to the television cameras, just like respectable politicians. Racists preached hatred over the internet. Economic inequality still existed, too. In the USA, a black American was twice as likely to be unemployed as a white.

Never give up

Rosa Parks may have been quiet and forgiving, but she was also tough and unswerving. She never gave up her ideals and still urged people onwards towards a fairer society. In 1977 Raymond, her husband, died of cancer and from 1979 she had to care for her elderly mother.

The year 1987 saw the founding of the Parks Institute, which encouraged young people to discover self-respect and confidence. In 1994 Rosa was mugged in her home by a young black intruder, but she battled on. In 1996 she was awarded the Presidential Medal of Freedom.

During her later years, Rosa Parks was helped through difficult times by her friend and fellow activist, Elaine Steel (left).

Rosa met Nelson Mandela in 1999. Mandela was a black
South African who had been jailed in 1964 for battling
against injustice in his own country. Not released until
1990, he became South Africa's first black, democratically
elected President in 1991.

Rosa died on 24th October 2005. She was the first
woman in American history to lie in state at the Capitol,
an honour usually given only to Presidents. Her
everlasting memorial will be her message – never give up
the struggle for freedom and justice.

Nelson Mandela (right) embraces Rosa Parks (centre) as the two
veteran campaigners meet in 1999.

Timeline

1500s   Start of the trans-Atlantic slave trade.

1807   Britain halts trans-Atlantic slave trade.

1833   Britain ends slavery in its empire (including Canada and the Caribbean). American Anti-Slavery Society calls for abolition in the USA.

1861-65 US Civil War, abolition of slavery.

1866   Founding of the Ku Klux Klan.

1884   Start of the 'Jim Crow' laws.

1909   Founding of the National Association for the Advancement of Coloured People (NAACP).

1913   *4 February:* Rosa Louise McCauley (Parks) is born.

1932   Rosa McCauley marries Raymond Parks.

1934   Founding of the Nation of Islam movement.

1941   USA enters the Second World War.

1955   *13 August:* the murder of Emmett Till.

        1 December: Rosa Parks is arrested for her bus protest.

1956   *13 November:* US Supreme Court rules against bus segregation laws.

        21 December: bus desegregation enforced in Montgomery, Alabama.

1957	*July:* death threats force Rosa Parks to move to Detroit.
	September: riots at Little Rock, Arkansas, as Black pupils try to enter high school.
1960	Lunch-counter sit-ins, Nashville, Tennessee.
1961	The 'Freedom Riders' challenge segregation.
1963	*12 June:* murder of Medgar Evers.
	23 June: Great March to Freedeom, Detroit.
	28 August: Martin Luther King addresses 300,000 in Washington, DC .
	22 November: assassination of President John F Kennedy.
1965	*21 February:* Malcolm X is assassinated in Harlem, New York.
	7 March: start of the Selma to Montgomery freedom march.
	August: violent riots in Watts, Los Angeles.
1966	Rise of the Black Panthers and the Black Power movement.
1967	*July:* violent riots in Detroit.
1968	*4 April:* assassination of Martin Luther King.
	5 June: assassination of Robert Kennedy.
1987	Founding of the Parks Institute.
1996	Rosa Parks is awarded the Presidential Medal of Freedom.
1999	Rosa Parks meets Nelson Mandela in Detroit.
2005	*24 October:* Rosa Parks dies, and lies in state at the Capitol.

Glossary

abolition Getting rid of a custom or law.

African Americans Americans whose ancestors came from Africa.

Black Power A movement calling for people of African descent to rise up and seize power for themselves.

boycott To make a protest by refusing to deal with someone or to use their services.

civil war A war between two armies within a single country, as happened with the USA 1861-65.

communist Believing that the working classes should seize power and take control of the economy and government.

discrimination Treating one group of people differently than another.

economic To do with the economy, the way in which money, employment and trade is organised.

harass To bother, or make trouble for someone.

immoral Offending against ideas of what is right or just.

integration Making sure that all people are included in something – the opposite of segregation.

intimidate To scare people off from doing something, to terrorise them.

jury A group of people called in to decide guilt or non-guilt in a court case.

Nobel Peace Prize An international prize that is awarded to people who have helped to make the world a more peaceful place.

pastor A clergyman, minister or priest.

plantation A large farming estate which produces a crop such as cotton or sugar cane.

race A group of people who are categorised by their physical appearance.

Index